# OSCAR WILDE

# OSCAR WILDE

## IN MEMORIAM
### (REMINISCENCES)

## *DE PROFUNDIS*

by ANDRÉ GIDE

*Translated from the French by*
BERNARD FRECHTMAN

PHILOSOPHICAL LIBRARY
*New York*

ISBN 978-0-8065-2970-7

PRINTED IN THE UNITED STATES OF AMERICA

# TRANSLATOR'S NOTE

THE PRESENT TRANSLATION INTRODUCES A WORK OF
Gide which dates from the first years of the century.
The first of the two essays was written in 1901; the
second, in 1905. They were published together in
1910 by Mercure de France.

The essays require no introductory comment.
However, the following two quotations from the
*Journal* supplement the text and provide interesting
perspectives. The first is dated January 1st, 1892,
when Gide was twenty-two years old; the second,
June 29th, 1913:

"Wilde has done me, I think, nothing but
harm. With him, I had forgotten how to think.
I had more varied emotions, but I could no
longer order them; I was particularly unable to
follow the deductions of others. A few thoughts,
occasionally; but my clumsiness in handling
them made me abandon them. I am now re-
suming, with difficulty, though with great de-
light, my history of philosophy, where I am
studying the problem of language (which I
shall resume with Muller and Renan)."

"Certainly, in my little book on Wilde, I appeared rather unfair toward his work and I pooh-poohed it too casually, I mean before having known it well enough. I admire, as I think back upon it, the good grace with which Wilde listened to me when, in Algiers, I passed judgment upon his plays (quite impertinently, as it seems to me now). No impatience in the tone of his reply, and not even a protest; it was then that he was led to say to me, "I have put all my genius into my life; I have put only my talent into my works." I should be curious to know whether he ever uttered this remark· to anyone else.

I do hope later on to be able to come back to the matter and tell everything which I dared not say at first. I would also like to *explain* Wilde's work in my own way, particularly his plays—whose chief interest lies between the lines."

B. F.

# FOREWORD

I WARN THE READER AT ONCE: THIS IS NEITHER A
biography of Oscar Wilde nor a study of his works;
it is the simple assembling of two sketches which
have not even the merit of being new, but which
the growing public of the great Irish poet has not
known where to find, since one of them remains
buried in a volume of various critical pieces,[1] and
the other has not yet been unearthed from a number
of *L'Ermitage* where I published it in August 1905.

Incapable of *re-writing* anything, I present both
of them again without changing a word in their
texts, though on at least one point my opinion has
been deeply modified: It seems to me today that in
my first essay I spoke of Oscar Wilde's work, and in
particular of his plays, with unjust severity. The
English as well as the French led me to do this, and
Wilde himself at times showed an amusing disdain
for his comedies by which I allowed myself to be
taken in. I admit that for a long time I therefore
believed that *An Ideal Husband* and *A Woman of
No Importance* were not to be regarded as anything
but dramatic entertainment which was itself "of no

[1] *Prétextes* (Mercure de France).

importance." To be sure, I have not come to consider these plays as perfect works; but they appear to me, today when I have learned to know them better, as among the most curious, the most significant and, whatever may have been said about them, the newest things in the contemporary theatre. If French criticism has already been surprised at the interest which it could take in the recent production of *Lady Windermere's Fan*, what would it not have thought of the other two plays!

In short, to him whose ears are sharp, *An Ideal Husband* and *A Woman of No Importance* reveal quite a bit about their author—as, for that matter, does each of his works. It might almost be said that the literary value of the latter is in direct proportion to their importance as confidences; and I still wonder that the climax should have held so little surprise in a life so strangely conscious, a life in which even the fortuitous seemed deliberate.

A. G.

# IN MEMORIAM

IT WAS A YEAR AGO THIS TIME,[1] IN BISKRA, THAT I
learned through the newspapers of the lamentable
end of Oscar Wilde. Distance did not permit me,
alas! to join the meagre cortège which followed his
remains to the cemetery of Bagneux; in vain did I
grieve that my absence seemed further to reduce
the small number of friends who had remained
faithful; the present pages, at least, I wanted to
write at once; but for a rather long time, Wilde's
name seemed again to become the property of the
newspapers . . . At present, now that all gossip
about this wretchedly famous name has quieted
down, now that the throng has grown weary, after
having praised, of being astonished and then of
damning, perhaps a friend may express a sadness
which persists, may bring, like a wreath to a forsaken grave, these pages of affection, admiration
and respectful pity.

When the scandalous trial, which excited English
opinion, threatened to wreck his life, a few men of
letters and a few artists attempted a kind of salvag-
ing in the name of literature and art. It was hoped

[1] Written in December 1901.

that by praising the writer, they might manage to exonerate the man. Alas! a misunderstanding arose; for we really must acknowledge that Wilde is not a great writer. Thus, all that was accomplished by the lead buoys which were thrown out to him was his ruin; his works, far from bearing him up, seemed to sink down with him. In vain did a few hands reach out to help. The wave of the world closed over him; all was over.

At the time, one could not at all think of defending him differently. Instead of trying to hide the man behind his work, the first thing to do was to show that the man was admirable, as I shall try to do today—the work itself then taking on an illumination. "I have put all my genius into my life; I have put only my talent into my works," said Wilde. A great writer, no, but a great *viveur*, if the word may be permitted to take on its full meaning. Like the philosophers of Greece, Wilde did not write but talked and lived his wisdom, imprudently entrusting it to the fluid memory of men, as if inscribing it on water. Let those who knew him longer tell the story of his life; one of those who listened to him most eagerly here simply sets down a few personal memories.

A. G.

# CONTENTS

### OSCAR WILDE'S *DE PROFUNDIS*

That religion and morals make such recommenda-
tions, well and good; but we are shocked to see
them set down in a code . . . I shall say as much
for the harsh measures taken to assure the rule of
our morals and manners. The most serious abuses
are less damaging than a system of inquisition
which degrades character.

—RENAN

# I

THOSE WHO CAME INTO CONTACT WITH WILDE ONLY
toward the end of his life have a poor notion, from
the weakened and broken being whom the prison
returned to us, of the prodigious being he was at
first. It was in '91 that I met him for the first time.
Wilde had at the time what Thackeray calls "the
chief gift of great men": success. His gesture, his
look triumphed. His success was so certain that it
seemed that it preceded Wilde and that all he
needed do was go forward to meet it. His books
astonished, charmed. His plays were to be the talk
of London. He was rich; he was tall; he was hand-
some; laden with good fortune and honors. Some
compared him to an Asiatic Bacchus; others to some
Roman emperor; others to Apollo himself—and the
fact is that he was radiant.

At Paris, no sooner did he arrive, than his name
ran from mouth to mouth; a few absurd anecdotes
were related about him: Wilde was still only the

man who smoked gold-tipped cigarettes and who walked about in the streets with a sunflower in his hand. For, Wilde, clever at duping the makers of worldly celebrity, knew how to project, beyond his real character, an amusing phantom which he played most spiritedly.

I heard him spoken of at the home of Mallarmé: he was portrayed as a brilliant talker, and I wished to know him, though I had no hope of managing to do so. A happy chance, or rather a friend, to whom I had told my desire, served me. Wilde was invited to dinner. It was at the restaurant. There were four of us, but Wilde was the only one who talked.

Wilde did not converse: he narrated. Throughout almost the whole of the meal, he did not stop narrating. He narrated gently, slowly; his very voice was wonderful. He knew French admirably, but he pretended to hunt about a bit for the words which he wanted to keep waiting. He had almost no accent, or at least only such as it pleased him to retain and which might give the words a sometimes new and strange aspect. He was fond of pronouncing *skepticisme* for "scepticisme" . . .[1] The

[1] The *sc* of *scepticisme* (scepticism) is pronounced as though it were *s* alone.—(Translator's note.)

tales which he kept telling us all through the evening were confused and not of his best; Wilde was uncertain of us and was testing us. Of his wisdom or indeed of his folly, he uttered only what he believed his hearer would relish; he served each, according to his appetite, his taste; those who expected nothing of him had nothing, or just a bit of light froth; and as his first concern was to amuse, many of those who thought they knew him knew only the jester in him.

When the meal was over, we left. As my two friends were walking together, Wilde took me aside:

"You listen with your eyes," he said to me rather abruptly. "That's why I'm going to tell you this story: When Narcissus died, the flowers of the field asked the river for some drops of water to weep for him. 'Oh!' answered the river, 'if all my drops of water were tears, I should not have enough to weep for Narcissus myself. I loved him!' 'Oh!' replied the flowers of the field, 'how could you not have loved Narcissus? He was beautiful.' 'Was he beautiful?' said the river. 'And who could know better than you? Each day, leaning over your bank, he beheld his beauty in your water . . .'"

Wilde paused for a moment . . .

" 'If I loved him,' replied the river, "it was because, when he leaned over my water, I saw the reflection of my waters in his eyes.' "

Then Wilde, swelling up with a strange burst of laughter, added, "That's called *The Disciple*."

We had arrived at his door and left him. He invited me to see him again. That year and the following year I saw him often and everywhere.

Before others, as I have said, Wilde wore a showy mask, designed to astonish, amuse, or, at times, exasperate. He never listened, and paid scant heed to ideas as soon as they were no longer his own. As soon as he ceased to shine all by himself, he effaced himself. After that, he was himself again only when one was once more alone with him.

But no sooner alone he would begin:

"What have you done since yesterday?"

And as my life at that time flowed along rather smoothly, the account that I might give of it offered no interest. I would docilely repeat trivial facts, noting, as I spoke, that Wilde's brow would darken.

"Is that really what you've done?"

"Yes," I would answer.

"And what you say is true!"

"Yes, quite true."

"But then why repeat it? You do see that it's not at all interesting. Understand that there are two worlds: the one that *is* without one's speaking about it; it's called the *real world* because there's no need to talk about it in order to see it. And the other is the world of art; that's the one which has to be talked about because it would not exist otherwise.

"There was once a man who was beloved in his village because he would tell stories. Every morning he left the village and in the evening when he returned, all the village workmen, after having drudged all day long, would gather about him and say, 'Come! Tell us! What did you see today?' He would tell: 'I saw a faun in the forest playing a flute, to whose music a troop of woodland creatures were dancing around.' 'Tell us more; what did you see?' said the men. 'When I came to the seashore, I saw three mermaids, at the edge of the waves, combing their green hair with a golden comb.' And the men loved him because he told them stories.

"One morning, as every morning, he left his village—but when he came to the seashore, lo! he beheld three mermaids combing their green hair with a golden comb. And as he continued his walk, he saw, as he came near the woods, a faun playing the flute to a troop of woodland creatures. That evening, when he came back to his village and was asked, as on other evenings, 'Come! Tell us! What did you see?' he answered, 'I saw nothing.' "

Wilde paused for some moments, let the effect of

the tale work its way in me, and then resumed, "I don't like your lips; they're straight, like those of someone who has never lied. I want to teach you to lie, so that your lips may become beautiful and twisted like those of an antique mask.

"Do you know what makes the work of art and what makes the work of nature? Do you know what makes them different? For, after all, the flower of the narcissus is as beautiful as a work of art—and what distinguishes them can not be beauty. Do you know what distinguishes them?—The work of art is always *unique*. Nature, which makes nothing durable, always repeats itself so that nothing which it makes may be lost. There are many narcissus flowers; that's why each one can live only a day. And each time that nature invents a new form, she at once repeats it. A sea-monster in a sea knows that in another sea is another sea-monster, his like. When God creates a Nero, a Borgia or a Napoleon in history, he puts another one elsewhere; this one is not known, it little matters; the important thing is that *one* succeed; for God invents man, and man invents the work of art.

"Yes, I know . . . one day there was a great uneasiness on earth, as if nature were at last going to create something unique, something truly unique—and Christ was born on earth. Yes, I know . . . but listen:

[6]

"When, in the evening, Joseph of Arimathaea went down from Mount Calvary where Jesus had just died he saw a young man seated on a white stone and weeping. And Joseph approached him and said, 'I understand that your grief is great, for certainly that Man was a just Man.' But the young man answered, 'Oh! that's not why I'm weeping. I'm weeping because I too have performed miracles! I too have restored sight to the blind, I have healed paralytics and I have raised up the dead. I too have withered the barren fig-tree and I have changed water into wine . . . And men have not crucified me.'"

And it seemed to me more than once that Oscar Wilde was convinced of his representative mission.

The Gospel disturbed and tormented the pagan Wilde. He did not forgive it its miracles. The pagan miracle is the work of art: Christianity was encroaching. All robust artistic unrealism requires an earnest realism in life.

His most ingenious apologues, his most disturbing ironies were designed to bring the two ethics face to face with one another, I mean pagan naturalism and Christian idealism, and to put the latter out of countenance.

"When Jesus wished to return to Nazareth," he

related, "Nazareth was so changed that He no longer recognized His city. The Nazareth in which He had lived had been full of lamentations and tears; this city was full of bursts of laughter and singing. And Christ, entering the city, saw slaves loaded with flowers hastening toward the marble stairway of a house of white marble. Christ entered the house, and at the rear of a room of jasper He saw lying on a regal couch a man whose disheveled hair was entwined with red roses and whose lips were red with wine. Christ approached him, touched him upon the shoulder and said, "Why leadest thou this life?' The man turned about, recognized Him and replied, 'I was a leper; Thou hast healed me. Why should I lead another life?'

"Christ went out of that house. And lo! in the street he beheld a woman whose face and garments were painted, and whose feet were shod with pearls; and behind her walked a man whose coat was of two colors and whose eyes were laden with desire. And Christ approached the man, touched him upon the shoulder and said, 'Why dost thou follow that woman and regard her thus?' The man, turning about, recognized Him and replied, 'I was blind; Thou hast healed me. What should I do otherwise with my sight?'

"And Christ approached the woman. 'The road which you follow,' He said to her, 'is that of sin;

wherefore follow it?' The woman recognized Him and laughingly said to Him, 'The road which I follow is a pleasing one and Thou hast pardoned me all my sins.'

"Then Christ felt His heart full of sadness and wished to leave that city. But as He was leaving it, He saw at length beside the moats of the city a youth who was weeping. Christ approached him, and touching his locks, said to him, 'My friend, wherefore weepest thou?'

"The youth lifted up his eyes, recognized Him, and replied, 'I was dead and Thou hast raised me up; what should I do otherwise with my life?' "

"Would you like me to tell you a secret?" Wilde began another day—it was at the home of Heredia; he had taken me aside in the midst of a crowded drawing-room—"a secret . . . but promise me not to tell it to anyone . . . Do you know why Christ did not love His mother?" This was spoken into my ear, in a low voice and as if ashamedly. He paused a moment, grasped my arm, drew back, and then bursting into laughter, said, "It's because she was a virgin! . . ."

Let me again be permitted to quote this tale, a most strange one and a tough nut for the mind to crack—it is a rare spirit that will understand the contradiction, which Wilde hardly seems to be inventing.

"... Then there was a great silence in the Chamber of God's Justice.—And the soul of the sinner advanced stark naked before God.

And God opened the book of the sinner's life:

'Certainly your life has been very bad: You have ... (followed a prodigious, marvelous enumeration of sins).[1]—Since you have done all that, I am certainly going to send you to Hell.'

'You can not send me to Hell.'

'And why can I not send you to Hell?'

'Because I have lived there all my life.'

Then there was a great silence in the Chamber of God's Justice.

'Well, since I can not send you to Hell, I am going to send you to Heaven.'

'You can not send me to Heaven.'

'And why can I not send you to Heaven?'

'Because I have never been able to imagine it.'

And there was a great silence in the Chamber of God's Justice." [2]

One morning Wilde handed me an article to read in which a rather dull-witted critic congratulated

---

[1] The written version which he later made of this tale is, for a wonder, excellent.

[2] Since Villiers de l'Isle-Adam betrayed it, everybody knows, alas! the "great secret of the Church": *There is no Purgatory.*

him for "knowing how to invent pleasant tales the better to clothe his thought."

"They believe," Wilde began, "that all thoughts are born naked . . . They don't understand that *I can not* think otherwise than in stories. The sculptor doesn't try to translate his thought into marble; *he thinks in marble,* directly.

"There was a man who could think only in bronze. And one day this man had an idea, the idea of joy, of the joy which dwells in the moment. And he felt that he had to tell it. But in all the world, not a single piece of bronze was left; for men had used it all. And this man felt that he would go mad if he did not tell his idea.

"And he thought about a piece of bronze on the grave of his wife, about a statue he had made to adorn the grave of his wife, of the only woman he had loved; it was the statue of sadness, of the sadness which dwells in life. And the man felt that he would go mad if he did not tell his idea.

"So he took the statue of sadness, of the sadness which dwells in life; he smashed it and made of it the statue of joy, of the joy which dwells only in the moment."

Wilde believed in some sort of fatality of the artist, and that the idea is stronger than the man.

"There are," he would say, "two kinds of artist: one brings answers, and the other, questions. We have to know whether one belongs to those who answer or to those who question; for the kind which questions is never that which answers. There are works which wait, and which one does not understand for a long time; the reason is that they bring answers to questions which have not yet been raised; for the question often arrives a terribly long time after the answer."

And he would also say:

"The soul is born old in the body; it is to rejuvenate it that the latter grows old. Plato is the youth of Socrates . . ."

Then I remained for three years without seeing him again.

# II

Here begin the tragic memories.

A persistent rumor, growing with each of his successes (in London he was being played at the same time in three theatres), ascribed strange practices to Wilde; some people were so kind as to take umbrage at them with a smile, and others took no umbrage at all; it was claimed moreover that he took no pains to hide them, that, on the contrary, he flaunted them; some said, courageously; others, cynically; others, affectedly. I listened to this rumor with great astonishment. Nothing, since I had been associating with Wilde, could have ever made me suspect a thing.—But already, out of prudence, a number of former friends were deserting him. People were not yet repudiating him outright, but they no longer made much of having met him.

An extraordinary chance brought our two paths together again. It was in January 1895. I was traveling; I was driven to do so by a kind of anxiety, more in quest of solitude than in the novelty of places. The weather was frightful; I had fled from Algiers toward Blidah; I was going to leave Blidah for Biskra. At the moment of leaving the hotel, out of idle curiosity, I looked at the blackboard where the names of the travelers were written. What did I see there?—Beside my name, touching it, that of Wilde . . . I have said that I was longing for solitude: I took the sponge and rubbed out my name.

Before reaching the station, I was no longer quite sure whether a bit of cowardice might not have been hidden in this act; at once, retracing my steps, I had my valise brought up again and rewrote my name on the board.

In the three years that I had not seen him (for I can not count a brief meeting at Florence the year before), Wilde had certainly changed. One felt less softness in his look, something raucous in his laughter and something frenzied in his joy. He seemed both more sure of pleasing and less ambitious to succeed in doing so; he was bolder, stronger, bigger. What was strange was that he no longer spoke in apologues; during the few days that I lingered in his company, I was unable to draw the slightest tale from him.

I was at first astonished at finding him in Algeria.

"Oh!" he said to me, "it's that now I'm fleeing from the work of art; I no longer want to adore anything but the sun . . . Have you noticed that the sun de-

[ 14 ]

tests thought; it always makes it withdraw and take refuge in the shade. At first, thought lived in Egypt; the sun conquered Egypt. It lived in Greece for a long time, the sun conquered Greece; then Italy and then France. At the present time, all thought finds itself pushed back to Norway and Russia, places where the sun never comes. The sun is jealous of the work of art."

To adore the sun, ah! was to adore life. Wilde's lyrical adoration was growing wild and terrible. A fatality was leading him on; he could not and would not elude it. He seemed to put all his concern, his virtue, into overexaggerating his destiny and losing patience with himself. He went to pleasure as one marches to duty.—"My duty to myself," he would say, "is to amuse myself terrifically."

Nietzsche astonished me less, later on, because I had heard Wilde say:

"Not happiness! Above all, not happiness. Pleasure! We must always want the most tragic . . ."

He would walk in the streets of Algiers, preceded, escorted, followed by an extraordinary band of ragamuffins; he chatted with each one; he regarded them all with joy and tossed his money to them haphazardly.

"I hope," he said to me, "to have quite demoralized this city."

I thought of the word used by Flaubert who,

when someone asked him what kind of glory he was
most ambitious of, replied, "That of demoralizer."

In the face of all this, I remained full of astonishment, admiration, and fear. I was aware of his shaky
situation, the hostilities, the attacks, and what a dark
anxiety he hid beneath his bold joy.[1] He spoke of

[1] One of those last Algiers evenings, Wilde seemed to have promised himself to say nothing serious. At length I grew somewhat irri-
tated with his too witty paradoxes:

"You've better things to say than witticisms," I began. "You're
talking to me this evening as if I were the public. You ought rather
talk to the public the way you know how to talk to your friends. Why
aren't your plays better? You talk away the best of yourself; why don't
you write it down?"

"Oh!" he exclaimed at once, "but my plays are not at all good; and
I don't put any stock in them at all. . . . But if you only knew what
amusement they give! . . . Almost every one is the result of a wager.
*Dorian Grey* too; I wrote it in a few days because one of my friends
claimed that I could never write a novel. It bores me so much,
writing!"—Then, suddenly bending over toward me: "Would you like
to know the great drama of my life?—It's that I've put my genius
into my life; I've put only my talent into my works."

It was only too true. The best of his writing is only a pale reflection of his brilliant conversation. Those who have heard him speak
find it disappointing to read him. *Dorian Grey*, at the very beginning,
was a splendid story, how superior to the *Peau de Chagrin!* how much
more *significant!* Alas! written down, what a masterpiece *manqué.*—
In his most charming tales there is too great an intrusion of literature.
Graceful as they may be, one feels too greatly the affectation; preci-
osity and euphuism conceal the beauty of the first invention; one feels
in them, one can never stop feeling, the three moments of their
genesis; the first idea is quite beautiful, simple, profound and certainly sensational; a kind of latent necessity holds its parts firmly
together; but from here on, the gift stops; the development of the
parts is carried out factitiously; they are not well organized; and
when, afterwards, Wilde works on his phrases, and goes about pointing them up, he does so by a prodigious overloading of concetti, of
trivial inventions, which are pleasing and curious, in which emotion
stops, with the result that the glittering of the surface makes our mind
lose sight of the deep central emotion.

returning to London; the Marquis of Q . . . was insulting him, summoning him, accusing him of flee-ing.

"But if you go back there, what will happen?" I asked him. "Do you know what you're risking?"

"One should never know that . . . They're ex-traordinary, my friends; they advise prudence. Pru-dence! But can I have any? That would be going backwards. I must go as far as possible . . . I can not go further . . . Something must happen . . . something else . . ."

Wilde embarked the following day.

The rest of the story is familiar. That "something else" was *hard labor.*[2]

[2] I have invented nothing and arranged nothing in the last re-marks I quote. Wilde's words are present to my mind, and I was going to say to my ear. I am not claiming that Wilde clearly saw prison rising up before him; but I do assert that the dramatic turn which surprised and astounded London, abruptly transforming Wilde from accuser to accused, did not, strictly speaking, cause him any surprise. The newspapers, which were unwilling to see anything more in him than a clown, did their best to misrepresent the attitude of his defense, to the point of depriving it of any meaning. Perhaps, in some far-off time it will be well to lift this frightful trial out of its abominable filth.

# III

As soon as he left prison, Oscar Wilde came back to France. At Berneval, a quiet little village in the neighborhood of Dieppe, a certain Sebastian Melmoth took up residence: it was he. As I had been the last of his French friends to see him, I wished to be the first to see him again. As soon as I could learn his address, I made haste.

I arrived toward the middle of the day. I arrived without having announced myself. Melmoth, whom the good cheer of Thaulow called rather often to Dieppe, was not to return until evening. He did not return until the middle of the night.

Winter was still lingering on. It was cold; it was ugly. All day long I roamed about the deserted beach, dejected and full of boredom. How could Wilde have chosen Berneval to live in? It was dismal.

Night came. I returned to take a room in the hotel, the same one in which Melmoth was living, and moreover the only one in the place. The hotel, clean, and agreeably situated, lodged only a few second-rate people, inoffensive associates in whose presence I had to dine. Sad society for Melmoth!

Luckily I had a book. Dismal evening! Eleven o'clock . . . I was going to give up waiting, when I heard the roll of a carriage . . . M. Melmoth had arrived.

M. Melmoth was chilled through and through. He had lost his overcoat on the way. A peacock feather which his servant had brought him the evening before (frightful omen) had presaged a misfortune; he was happy that it was not that. But he was shivering and the whole hotel was excited about getting a grog heated for him. He hardly said hello to me. Before the others at least, he did not want to seem moved. And my emotion almost at once subsided at finding Sebastian Melmoth so simply like the Oscar Wilde that he had been: no longer the lyrical madman of Algeria, but the gentle Wilde of before the crisis; and I found myself carried back not two years, but four or five years earlier; the same worn look, the same amused laugh, the same voice . . .

He occupied two rooms, the two best in the hotel, and had had them tastefully arranged. Many books on the table, and among them he showed me my *Nourritures Terrestres* which had recently been published. A pretty Gothic Virgin, on a high pedestal, in the shadow . . .

We were sitting near the lamp and Wilde was sipping his grog. I noticed then, in the better light, that the skin of his face had become red and common; that of the hands even more so, though they were again wearing the same rings; one, which he was very fond of, had a setting of an Egyptian scarab in lapis-lazuli. His teeth were atrociously decayed. We chatted. I spoke to him again of our last meeting in Algiers. I asked him whether he remembered that at the time he had almost predicted the catastrophe.

"Isn't it so," I said, "that you knew to a certain extent what was in store for you in England; you had foreseen the danger and rushed into it? . . ."

(Here I do not think that I can do better than recopy the pages in which I transcribed, a short time later, everything that I could recall of what he had said.)

"Oh! of course! of course, I knew that there would be a catastrophe—that one or another, I was expecting it. It had to end that way. Just imagine: it wasn't possible to go any further; and it couldn't last. That's why, you see, it has to be ended. Prison has completely changed me. I counted on it for that.— B . . . is terrible; he can't understand it; he can't understand my not going back to the same existence; he accuses the others of having changed me . . . But one should never go back to the same existence

. . . My life is like a work of art; an artist never starts the same thing twice . . . or if he does, it's that he hasn't succeeded. My life before prison was as successful as possible. Now it's something that's over."

He lit a cigarette.

"The public is so dreadful that it never knows a man except by the last thing that he's done. If I went back to Paris now, all they'd want to see in me is the . . . convict. I don't want to reappear before writing a play. I must be let alone until then."— And he added abruptly, "Haven't I done well to come here? My friends wanted me to go to the Midi to rest; because, at the beginning, I was very tired. But I asked them to find me, in the North of France, a very small beach, where I wouldn't see anyone, where it's quite eold, where it's almost never sunny . . . Oh! haven't I done well to come and live in Berneval?" (Outside the weather was frightful.)

"Here everyone is very good to me. The *curé* in particular. I'm so fond of the little church! Would you believe that it's called Notre Dame de Liesse! Aoh! isn't it charming?—And now I know that I'm never again going to be able to leave Berneval, because this morning the *curé* offered me a permanent stall in the choir!

"And the customs officers! They were so bored here! so I asked them whether they hadn't anything to read; and now I'm bringing them all the novels of Dumas the elder . . . I have to stay here, don't I?

"And the children! aaah! they adore me! The day of the queen's jubilee, I gave a great festival, a great dinner, to which I had forty school-children—all! all! with the teacher! to fête the queen! Isn't that absolutely charming? . . . You know I'm very fond of the queen. I always have her portrait with me." And he showed me, pinned to the wall, the portrait by Nicholson.

I got up to look at it; a small library was nearby; I looked at the books for a moment. I should have liked to get Wilde to talk to me more seriously. I sat down again, and with a bit of fear I asked him whether he had read *The House of the Dead*. He did not answer directly but began:

"The writers of Russia are extraordinary. What makes their books so great is the pity which they've put into them. At first, I liked *Madame Bovary* a great deal, didn't I; but Flaubert didn't want any pity in his work, and that's why it seems small and closed; pity is the side on which a work is open, by which it appears infinite . . . Do you know, dear,[1] that it's pity that kept me from killing myself? Oh! during the first six months I was terribly unhappy; so unhappy that I wanted to kill myself; but what

[1] This term, which may here seem unexpected to the reader, appears in English in the original text. (Translator's note.)

kept me from doing so was looking at *the others,* seeing that they were as unhappy as I, and having pity. O dear! it's an admirable thing, pity; and I didn't know what it was! (He was speaking in an almost low voice, without any exaltation.) Have you quite understood how admirable a thing pity is? As for me, I thank God each evening—yes, on my knees, I thank God for making me know what it is. For I entered prison with a heart of stone, thinking only of my pleasure, but now my heart has been completely broken; pity has entered my heart; I now understand that pity is the greatest, the most beautiful thing that there is in the world . . . And that's why I can't be angry with those who condemned me, nor with anyone, because without them I would not have known all that.—B . . . writes me terrible letters; he tells me that he doesn't understand me; that he doesn't understand that I'm not angry with everyone; that everyone has been hateful to me . . . No, he doesn't understand me; he can't understand me any more. But I repeat to him in each letter: we can not follow the same path; he has his; it's very beautiful; I have mine. His is that of Alcibiades; mine is now that of Saint Francis of Assisi . . . Are you familiar with Saint Francis of Assisi? aoh! wonderful! wonderful! Do you want to do something very nice for me? Send me the best life of Saint Francis that you know . . ."

I promised him to do so; he continued:

"Yes—then we had a charming warden, aoh! quite charming! but the first six months I was terribly unhappy. There was a very nasty warden, a German, who was very cruel because he was completely lacking in imagination." This last remark, said very fast, was irresistibly comical, and as I burst out laughing, he laughed too, repeated it, and then continued:

"He didn't know what to imagine to make us suffer . . . You'll see how lacking he was in imagination . . . You have to know that in prison you're allowed to go outside only an hour a day; you then walk around a court behind one another, and it's absolutely forbidden to speak to one another. There are guards watching you and there are terrible punishments for the one they catch.—Those who are in prison for the first time can be recognized by their not knowing how to speak without moving their lips . . . I had already been locked up six weeks and hadn't yet said a word to anybody—to anybody. One evening we were walking behind one another that way during the recreation hour, and suddenly, behind me, I heard my name uttered: it was the prisoner behind me who was saying, 'Oscar Wilde, I pity you because you must be suffering more than we.' So I made an enormous effort not to be noticed (I thought I was going to faint), and I said without turning around, 'No, my friend, we are all suffering equally.'—and that day I no longer had any desire to kill myself.

"We talked like that for several days. I knew his name and what he did. His name was P . . .; he was an excellent chap; aoh! excellent! . . . But I still didn't know how to talk without moving my lips, and one evening: 'C.33! (C.33, that was I)— C.33 and C.48, step out of line!' So we stepped out of line and the guard said, "You're going to be brought up before the warden."—And as pity had already entered my heart, I was afraid only for him; indeed, I was happy to suffer because of him.—But the warden was quite terrible. He had P . . . brought in first; he wanted to question us separately —because you have to know that the penalty for the one who starts speaking and the one who answers is not the same; the penalty of the one who speaks first is double that of the other; ordinarily, the first gets two weeks of solitary confinement, the second, only one; so the warden wanted to know which of us two had spoken first, and, of course, P . . ., who was an excellent chap, said that it was he. And, when, afterward, the warden sent for me to question me, of course I said that it was I. The warden then got very red, because he no longer understood.—'But P . . . also says that he's the one who started! I can't understand . . .'

"Imagine that, dear!! He couldn't understand! He was very embarrassed; he kept saying, 'But I gave *him* two weeks . . .' and then he added, 'All right, if that's how things stand, I'm going to give both of you two weeks.' Isn't that extraordinary! That man had no sort of imagination."

Wilde was enormously amused at what he was saying; he was laughing; he was happy to be telling a story:

"And naturally, after the two weeks, we had a greater desire to talk to one another than before. You don't know how sweet that can seem, to feel that we were suffering for each other.—Little by little, as we weren't in the same line every day, little by little I was able to speak to each of the others; to all! to all! . . . I knew each one's name, each one's history, and when he was to leave prison . . . And to each one of them I would say, 'When you get out of prison, the first thing you're to do is to go to the post-office; there will be a letter for you with some money.'—With the result that, in that way, I continue to know them, because I love them very much. And some of them are quite delightful. Would you believe that already three of them have come to see me here! Isn't that quite wonderful? . . .

"The one who replaced the nasty warden was a very charming man, aoh! remarkable! quite pleasant to me . . . And you can't imagine how much good it did me in prison that *Salomé* was being played in Paris precisely at that time. Here it had been completely forgotten that I was a man of letters! When they saw here that my play was a success in Paris, they said to themselves, 'Well! that's certainly strange! so he has talent.' And from that moment on, I was allowed to read all the books I liked.

"I thought at first that what would please me most would be Greek literature. I asked for Sophocles, but I couldn't take to it. Then I thought of the Church Fathers; but they didn't interest me either. And all at once, I thought of Dante . . . oh! Dante! I read Dante every day; in Italian; I read him all through; but neither the *Purgatory* nor the *Paradise* seemed to be written for me. It was his *Inferno* especially that I read; how could I have helped loving it? We were *in* Hell. Hell was the prison . . ."

That same evening he told me his plan for a drama about Pharaoh and an ingenious story about Judas.

The next day he took me into a charming little house, two hundred yards from the hotel, which he had rented and was beginning to have furnished; it was there that he wanted to write his dramas, first his *Pharaoh*, then an *Ahab and Jezebel* (he pronounced it *Isabel*), which he related marvelously.

The carriage which was taking me away was harnessed. Wilde got into it with me, to accompany me a moment. He spoke to me again about my book and praised it, but with a certain indefinable reticence. Finally the carriage came to a stop. He said farewell to me, started to get off, but suddenly, "Listen, dear, you've got to make me a promise now. *Les Nourritures terrestres* is fine . . . it's very fine . . . But dear, promise me: from now on don't ever write *I* any more."

And as I appeared not quite to understand him, he went on, "In art, don't you see, there is no *first* person."

# IV

When I was back in Paris, I went to tell B . . . what was happening to him. B . . . said to me, "But that's all utterly ridiculous. He's quite incapable of putting up with boredom. I know him very well: he writes to me every day; and it's my opinion too that first he has to finish his play; but afterwards, he'll come back to me; he's never done anything good in solitude; he constantly needs distraction. All the best things that he's written were written when he was with me.—Just look at his last letter . . ." B . . . showed it to me and read it to me.—It begged B . . . to let him finish his *Pharaoh* in peace, but said, in effect, that, once the play was written, he would come back, would join him again—and ended with this glorious phrase: ". . . and then I shall again be *the King of Life.*"

# V

AND SHORTLY AFTERWARD, WILDE CAME BACK TO Paris.[1] His play was not written; it never will be. Society knows quite well how to go about it when it wants to dispose of a man, and knows means subtler than death . . . For two years Wilde had suffered too much and too passively. His will had been broken. The first months, he could still delude himself, but he very soon gave way. It was like an abdication. Nothing remained in his shattered life but the mournful musty odor of what he had once been; a need every now and then to prove that he was still thinking; wit, but artificial, forced, crumpled. I saw him again only twice.

One evening, on the boulevards, when I was strolling with G . . ., I heard my name called. I turned about: it was Wilde. Ah! how changed he was! . . . "If I reappeared before having written

[1] The representatives of his family assured Wilde that they would make things comfortable for him if he agreed to undertake certain engagements, among others that of never seeing B . . . again. He could not or would not undertake them.

my drama, the world would insist on seeing only the convict in me," he had said to me. He had reappeared without the drama, and, as a few people had shut their doors to him, he no longer tried to return anywhere; he roamed about. Friends, again and again, had tried to save him; they used all their ingenuity, they took him to Italy . . . Wilde very quickly escaped; relapsed. Among those remaining faithful the longest, some had repeated to me so often that "Wilde was no longer fit to be seen". . . I was somewhat ill at ease, I confess, at seeing him again in a place where so many people might be passing by.—Wilde was sitting at a table on the terrace of a café. He ordered two cocktails for G . . . and me . . . I was going to sit down facing him, that is, in such a way as to turn my back to the passers-by, but Wilde, perturbed by this gesture, which he thought was due to an absurd shame (he was not, alas! completely mistaken):

"Oh! sit down here, near me," he said, pointing to a chair beside him; "I'm so alone these days!"

Wilde was still well dressed; but his hat was no longer so glossy; his collar had the same shape, but it was no longer so clean; the sleeves of his frock-coat were slightly frayed.

"When, in times gone by, I used to meet Verlaine, I didn't blush for him," he went on, with an attempt at pride. "I was rich, joyful, covered with glory, but

I felt that to be seen near him did me honor, even when Verlaine was drunk . . ." Then, afraid of boring G . . ., I think, he abruptly changed his tone, tried to be witty, to joke, and became dismal. My recollection here remains abominably painful. Finally, my friend and I got up. Wilde insisted upon paying for the drinks. I was going to say good-bye to him when he took me aside and, confusedly, in a low voice, "Look," he said, "you've got to know . . . I'm absolutely without resources . . ."

A few days later, for the last time, I saw him again. I want to quote only a word of our conversation. He had told me of his difficulties, of the impossibility of continuing, of beginning a task. Sadly I reminded him of the promise he had made himself not to reappear in Paris except with a finished play:

"Ah!" I began, "why have you left Berneval so soon, when you were supposed to stay there for such a long time? I can't say that I'm angry with you, but . . ."

He interrupted me, put his hand on mine, looked at me with his most dismal look:

"One shouldn't be angry," he said to me, "with *someone who has been struck.*"

This last interview is of 1898; I left shortly afterward to travel and never again saw Oscar Wilde who died only two years later. Robert Ross, his faithful friend, has just given to the public a few highly interesting documents which shed light on the poet's last days. He appears to us there less alone, less forsaken than my account led one to suppose. The devotion of Reginald Turner in particular, who watched over him those last days, did not slacken for a moment.

Following this publication, certain German or English papers accused me of having tried to stylize my last recollections, of taking pleasure in forcing the antithesis between the triumphant "King of Life" of the glorious days and the pitiful Sebastian Melmoth of the dark days.

Everything I have related is simply and strictly accurate. Historical truth, insofar as one can achieve it, has always seemed to me infinitely more moving and far richer in meaning than the romantic element that might be drawn from it. The precious information of Mr. Ross completes mine and is a continuation of it, and moreover it is not he who has ever tried to oppose them to one another. His is of 1900 and mine of 1898, a period in which Wilde, little or poorly befriended, was letting himself go.

Howbeit, here is the letter which I wrote, already some years ago, to Mr. X . . . who, likewise, thought that he had found a certain contradiction between my account and the recognition of that generous fidelity from which certain friends never departed:

"As far the pecuniary question goes, Lord Alfred Douglas' explanation is the only plausible one—I believe, in effect, that Wilde, on leaving prison, would have had enough to live on tolerably well, if he had not been 'incurably extravagant and reckless.' But it is none the less true that, the last times I saw Wilde, he seemed deeply miserable, sad, impotent and hopeless—as, in fact, he is portrayed, for example,

[ 33 ]

in this letter which he wrote to me a short time before he left for Cannes (winter of '97-98), and which I cite, however beautiful it may be, only to help you set things straight:

'. . . *However, at the present moment I am very sad—I have received nothing from my publisher in London who owes me money: and I am in extreme want . . . You see how wretched the tragedy of my life has become—suffering is possible—is perhaps necessary—but poverty, destitution— that's what's terrible. It soils man's soul . . .*

Howbeit, I should be deeply grieved that something in my article might in any way have displeased Lord Alfred who conducted himself in that whole affair with the greatest nobility, as I shall one day set down in writing, and for whom I have retained a keen affection. Be so good as to tell him that if you see him again . . ."

In the space of a few months, two of Wilde's books have just been published in our language: *Intentions* [1] and *De Profundis;* [2] the first dates from the most brilliant period of his success; the second, dated from prison, stands facing it, seems its antithesis or palinode. I should have liked, in this article, not to separate these two books, to discover one in the other, the memory of the first in the second, and, especially, the promises of the second in the first. But

[1] Oscar Wilde, *Intentions*, translated by J.-Joseph Renaud, 1 vol. in-18. (P.-V. Stock). There has since appeared a much better translation by M. Charles Grolleau with a preface by Hugues Rebell (Carrington).

[2] Oscar Wilde, *De Profundis*, preceded by letters written from prison, and followed by the *Ballad of Reading Gaol*, translated by Henry-D. Davray, 1 vol. in-18 (Mercure de France).

Michel Arnauld, in this very place,[3] has spoken of *Intentions* too excellently for me to have to recur to it; I refer the reader to the high praise he has given this most remarkable book and turn to *De Profundis*.

*De Profundis* can hardly be considered as a book; it is, disengaged from some rather vain and specious theories, the sobbing of a wounded man who is struggling. I was unable to listen to it without tears; I should like, however, to speak of it without any trembling in my voice.

*"Life cheats us with shadows,"* wrote Wilde six years before his trial. *"We ask it for pleasure. It gives it to us, with bitterness and disappointment in its train."*

*And further on: "Life! Life! Don't let us go to life for our fulfillments or our experience. It is a thing narrowed by circumstances, incoherent in its utterance, and without that fine correspondence of form and spirit which is the only thing that can satisfy the artistic and critical temperament. It makes us pay too high a price for its wares, and we purchase the meanest of its secrets at a cost that is monstrous and infinite."*

What, at least, is this mean secret that Wilde, experienced as he nevertheless was, had to purchase at so monstrous a price?—From page to page, in his *De Profundis*, he repeats it: *"That something hid-*

[3] *Ermitage* of April 15th, 1905.

[ 35 ]

*den away in my nature, like a treasure in a field, is humility."* That was not perhaps what the essayist was seeking; but what is to be done about it? For the present, he must cling to it since that is all he has. *"There is only one thing for me now, absolute humility."* And if at first he calls his state *a horrible disgrace,* shortly afterwards, regaining his self-possession, or pretending to regain his self-possession, he writes: *"It is the last thing left in me, and the best: the ultimate discovery at which I have arrived, the starting-point for a fresh development . . ."* When, in the case of an artist, for external or inner reasons, the creative spring runs dry, the artist settles down, renounces and makes of his weariness a wisdom which he calls: having found the Truth. For Tolstoi, as for Wilde, this "truth" is approximately the same—and how could it be otherwise?

*"The starting-point for a fresh development!"* . . . My mind is made up: I shall mix my voice as little as possible with Wilde's, that is, shall, as often as possible, content myself with quoting him; the sentences which I shall extract from the book will illuminate it better than anything I might say about it.

*"I hope to be able to recreate my creative faculty,"* writes Wilde desperately. While waiting, he covers over the only retreat left to him with all the sophistries that he can muster: *"I have got to make every-*

*thing that has happened to me good for me. The plank bed, the loathsome food, the hard ropes shredded into oakum till one's finger-tips grow dull with pain, the menial offices with which each day begins and finishes, the harsh orders that routine seems to necessitate, the dreadful dress that makes sorrow grotesque to look at, the silence, the solitude, the shame—each and all of these things I have to transform into a spiritual experience. There is not a single degradation of the body which I must not try and make into a spiritualising of the soul."* And again: *"Whatever is realised is right."* And finally: *"While for the first year of my imprisonment I did nothing else, and can remember nothing else, but wring my hands in impotent despair, and say, 'What an ending, what an appalling ending!' now I try to say to myself, and sometimes when I am not torturing myself do really and sincerely say, 'What a beginning, what a wonderful beginning!' It may really be so. It may become so."* Then without quite realizing, or admitting to himself, that he is going cruelly counter to that "absolute humility" which he is extolling: *"In the very fact that people will recognize me wherever I go and know all about my life, as far as its follies go, I can discern something good for me. It will force on me the necessity of again asserting myself as an artist, and as soon as I possibly can. If I can produce only one beautiful work of art I shall be able to rob malice of its venom, and cowardice of its sneer, and to pluck out the tongue of scorn by the roots."*

*"I feel,"* he goes on to say, *"that not to be ashamed of having been punished is one of the first points I must attain to, for the sake of my own imperfection, and because I am so imperfect.*

*"Then I must learn to be happy. Once I knew it, or thought I knew it, by instinct . . . Now I am approaching life from a completely new standpoint, and even to conceive happiness is often extremely difficult for me."* Then elsewhere: *"And if I am not ashamed of my punishment, as I hope not to be, I shall be able to think, and walk, and live with freedom."*

For those who knew Wilde before and then after prison, such words remain doubtfully painful; for his artistic silence was not the pious silence of a Racine, and *humility* was only a pompous name that he gave to his impotence. *"Many men on their release carry their prison about with them into the air, and hide it as a secret disgrace in their hearts, and at length, like poor poisoned things, creep into some hole and die."* —"Like a poisoned thing," yes, that is quite how I here see the tremendous Wilde; no longer the brilliant conqueror whom society, about to sacrifice him, cajoled, alas, but mottled, deformed, tired; wandering like Peter Schlemihl in quest of his shadow, heavy and lamentable, and saying to me with an attempt at laughter which sounded like a sob: *"They have taken away my soul; I don't know what they've done with it."*

From the depth of his "humility," the bursts of his former pride are even more dismal: *"I am not prepared,"* he announces, *"to sit in the grotesque pillory they put me into, for all time; for the simple reason that I inherited from my father and mother a name of high distinction in literature and art, and I can not for eternity allow that name to be degraded."*—*"She and my father,"* he announces again, *"had bequeathed me a name they had made noble and honoured . . . I had disgraced that name eternally. I had made it a low byword among low people. I had dragged it through the very mire . . . What I suffered then, and still suffer, is not for pen to write."* Elsewhere, he is preoccupied with acting *"as a gentleman by bowing my head and accepting everything."*

Wilde, still strangely lucid, when, however, he did not attempt to give himself illusions about the failure of his pride, was not mistaken about the nature of his fault: it was out of a deficiency of individualism, not out of an excess of individualism, that he had succumbed. *"People used to say of me that I was too individualistic . . . Indeed, my ruin*

*came not from too great individualism of life, but
from too little. The one disgraceful, unpardonable,
and to all time contemptible action of my life was to
allow myself to appeal to society for help and protection."* We all know the story: it was *he* who
brought action against the most illustrious of his de-
famers and entered as accuser into "that chamber
of men's justice" . . . False boldness, ignorance,
folly! I imagine a Byron thus appealing to the society which he was braving . . . *"Of course,"* he
continues, *"once I had put into motion the forces of
society, society turned on me and said, 'Have you
been living all this time in defiance of my laws, and
do you now appeal to these laws for protection?
You should have those laws exercised to the full. You
shall abide by what you have appealed to.' The result is that I am in gaol."*

Yes, a deficiency of individualism, and that is why
what he blushes at is not what society accuses him
of, his "sins," but at having allowed himself to be
caught in such an unfavorable position; *"I don't regret for a single moment having lived for pleasure.
I did it to the full, as one should do everything that
one does."* Yes, a deficiency of individualism, hence
this exasperation. *"Everything about my tragedy
has been hideous, mean, repellant, lacking in style."*
Or: *"Certainly no man ever fell so ignobly, and by
such ignoble instruments, as I did."* Or again: *"In-*

*deed my entire tragedy seems to me grotesque and nothing else."*—Certainly it was not for him, it is for us to perceive its grandeur. The prison, which yesterday was his shame, magnifies him and today gives his tragic figure an importance which could not have been loaned for long to this playboy of genius by the footlights of the London drawing-rooms and stages where he paraded.

From the depth of his dungeon, he is astounded as he recalls that departed splendor, that glory which he hardly exaggerates; he is astounded as he now recounts it to himself. *"The gods had given me almost everything,"* he cries.

*"Few men held such a position in their own lifetime, and have it so acknowledged."* His tongue seems to play over the slight taste of honey that remains on his lips. *"I used to live entirely for pleasure,"* he writes, and elsewhere: *"I filled my life to the very brim with pleasure, as one might fill a cup to the very brim with wine."*

But through the excess of pleasure, I admire the secret advance toward a more significant destiny. As he becomes less wilful, he becomes more representative. This fatality was leading him on as if there were something exemplary about it; he sometimes abandoned himself to it without making any further effort to misinterpret it: *"To have continued the same life would have been wrong because it would have been limiting. I had to pass on."* This latent fatality, if I may say so, makes the beauty, the unity of his life, and intimately illuminates his work. Yes, the work of him for whom to "conceal the artist" was "art's aim" becomes for us, as it were, confidential. *"Of course all this is foreshadowed and prefigured in my books,"* and he cites them one after the other in succession, and finally: *"the prose poem of the man who from the bronze of the image of the 'Pleasure that liveth for a moment' has to make the image of the 'Sorrow that abideth forever' . . . "* Alas! alas! poor Wilde, that was not what your story said; quite the contrary, the artist of whom you speak smashed the statue of Grief in order to make of it that of Joy; and your wilful error remains more eloquent than an avowal.

That is why I can not help feeling a certain irritation, upon reading in the preface which M. Joseph Renaud joins to his translation of *Intentions:* "These facts, imperfectly established, be it noted, which cast into prison a writer who was glorious, rich, and esteemed by all, prove nothing against his work. Let us forget them . . . Do we not read, despite their private lives, Musset, Baudelaire, etc.? If someone were to reveal that Flaubert and Balzac had committed crimes, would we have to burn *Salammbo* and *Cousine Bette?* etc. . . . The works belong to us, not the authors."—Are we still worrying about that sort of thing! Doubtless these gracious words are said with the best intention in the world, but does not Wilde himself tell us in *De Profundis:* "*A great friend of mine—a friend of ten years' standing —came to see me some time ago, and told me that he did not believe a single word of what was said against me, and wished me to know that he considered me quite innocent, and the victim of a hideous plot. I burst into tears at what he said, and told him that while there was much amongst the definite charges that was quite untrue and transferred to me by revolting malice, still that my life had been full of perverse pleasures, and that unless he accepted that as a fact about me and realized it to the full I could not possibly be friends with him any more, or ever be in his company.*" And elsewhere: "*To regret one's own experiences is to arrest one's own development. To deny one's own experiences is to put a lie into the lips of one's own life. It is no less than a denial of the soul.*"

What is the use of claiming that "if Flaubert had committed crimes," *Salammbo* would not interest us any the less; how much more interesting and right it is to understand that "if Flaubert had committed crimes" it is not *Salammbo* that he would have written, but . . . something else, or nothing at all; and that if Balzac had wanted to *live* his *Comédie humaine,* that might have prevented him from writing it.—Wilde was in the habit of saying that "everything that is gained for life is lost for art," and that is the very reason why Wilde's life is tragic. —"*Must we go, then, to Art for everything?*" he has one of the speakers say in the best dialogue in *Intentions*. "*For everything,*" replies the second. "*Because Art does not hurt us.*"

No, in order to read his work better, regardless of what M. Joseph Renaud says about it, let us not pretend to ignore the drama of the man who, though knowing that it wounds, wished, nevertheless, *to address himself to life;* who, after having taught in so masterly a way that "*Art begins where imitation ends,*" that "*Life is the solvent that breaks up Art, the enemy that lays waste the house,*" and finally that "*Life imitates Art far more than Art imitates Life,*" offered himself as an example, and, with his own life gave, as it were, a *proof ad absurdum* of his words—quite like the hero of one of his most beautiful poems, like that man who was a clever storyteller, who every evening charmed the people of his village by relating the marvelous adventures which he pretended to have had during the day, but who, the day when some tragic adventure *in reality* befell him, could find nothing more to say.

M. Davray prefixes to his translation of *De Profundis* four letters written from prison which the

English edition does not contain; [4] some pages of these letters are so pathetic and have so urgent a psychological interest that I can hardly refrain from copying them here. [5] I would like to quote the whole book; better to refer the reader to it—and to consider myself satisfied if I have been able, be it ever so little, to be of service to a sad and glorious memory, for which it is time to cease having only contempt, insolent indulgence, or pity even more insulting than contempt.

[4] Translator's note: These letters appear in later editions.

[5] I prefer to quote the passage from *De Profundis* which the English publisher had good reasons for not giving. (See Appendix.)

## APPENDIX

"Other miserable men when they are thrown into prison, if they are robbed of the beauty of the world are at least safe in some measure from the world's most deadly slings, most awful arrows. They can hide in the darkness of their cells and of their very disgrace make a mode of sanctuary. The world having had its will goes its way, and they are left to suffer undisturbed. With me it has been different. Sorrow after sorrow has come beating at the prison doors in search of me; they have opened the gates wide and let them in. Hardly if at all have my friends been suffered to see me. But my enemies have had full access to me always; twice in my public appearances in the Bankruptcy Court; twice again in my public transferences from one prison to another have I been shown under conditions of unspeakable humiliation to the gaze and mockery of men. The messenger of Death has brought me his tidings and gone his way; and in entire solitude and isolated from all that could give me comfort or suggest relief I have had to bear the intolerable burden of misery and remorse, which the memory of my mother placed upon me and places upon me still.

Hardly has that wound been dulled, not healed, by time, when violent and bitter and harsh letters come to me from solicitors. I am at once taunted and threatened with poverty. That I can bear. I can school myself to worse than that; but my two children are taken from me by legal procedure. That is, and always will remain to me a source of infinite distress, of infinite pain, of grief without end or limit. That the law should decide and take upon itself to decide that I am one unfit to be with my own children is something quite horrible to me. The disgrace of prison is as nothing compared with it. I envy the other men who tread the yard along with me. I am sure that their children wait for them, look for their coming, will be sweet to them.

The poor are wiser, more charitable, more kind, more sensitive than we are."

# INDEX

# OSCAR WILDE

CPSIA information can be obtained
at www.ICGtesting.com
Printed in the USA
BVHW071919090221
599682BV00002B/154